CHANNELLED ANGEL MESSAGES.

A Pocket book for a better life.

Angels / L. Marsh

XXX

ANGELS /L. MARSH

Copyright © 2016 Laura Marsh.

First Published 2016.

All rights reserved.

No part of this book can be reproduced without the consernt of the copyright holder. Laura Marsh.

Laura Marsh has asserted her right under the Copyright, Designs and Patents Act 1998 to be identified as the author of this work.

ISBN:10:1539567028

ISBN-13:9781539567028

CONTENTS

Part 1. Channelled help from the Angels.

1.	You are safe, loved and never alone.	Pg 21
2.	Raising your vibration.	Pg 26
3.	You have it all there.	Pg 28
4.	Channelling.	Pg 31
5.	Manifesting and The Law of Attraction.	Pg 36
6.	Healing.	Pg 41
7.	Addiction.	Pg 45
8.	Time for you.	Pg 52
9.	Your Empowerment.	Pg 62
10.	Love.	Pg 70

11.	Fear & Worry.	Pg 77
12.	Illness.	Pg 90
13.	Goals & Dreams.	Pg 96
14.	Freedom.	Pg 102
15.	Security.	Pg 109
16.	Trust.	Pg 112
17.	Sex.	Pg 118
18.	Death, Bereavement & Eternity.	Pg 123
19.	Body & Body Image.	Pg 128
20.	Forgiveness.	Pg 138
21.	Success.	Pg 143
22.	Happiness & Joy.	Pg 149
23.	Affirmations.	Pg 160

24. Receiving Good Things.   Pg 167

25 Bringing peace to the   Pg 176
    world.

Part 2. Q & A. Channelled answers to some of your big questions from the Angels.

For You

Take a deep breath... YOU are not alone.

Take another deep breath... And now another....

Ask us Angels to be with you, now... And we ARE immediately with you, giving you all the love and comfort you need.

All the time and every time!

In our fast paced modern world, I feel a need to bring you access to channelled Angel messages to help you live happier lives.

My only desire is for you to be happy, empowered, and able to heal the challenges that present themselves to you. This is the help you have requested, help from the Angels. With my love and theirs. X

WE ANGELS ARE NOT LINKED TO ANY RELIGION. FOR HUMANITY IS ONE. WE ALL HAVE ACCESS TO INFINITE LOVE AND WISDOM. EACH AND EVERY ONE OF US HAS ACCESS TO ANGELIC LOVE AND GUIDANCE 24/7.

THIS IS OUR GIFT TO YOU. X

There is no coincidence in this being channelled, just before the holidays. This time can leave many of you feeling isolated and lonely. Know you are never alone. You are always loved. You sitting there in front of you modern technology connected to a world wide web, connecting all of you beautiful souls together. Just think how many of you are out there and ask yourself, Am I ever alone?

If you want to be in the company of others, just ask us Angels to bring friends to you, do not feel lack in your hearts, feel love! Say "Please bring me a friend now, let a neighbour knock or let the phone ring, but please bring me a friend now." Wait and see what miracle will come to you! With love from your Angels. X

16

What are Angels?

Angels are messengers between our world and heaven. They are beings of purity, light, wisdom, healing, positivity and love.

Each person has their own Guardian Angel, who has been with their soul, for all incarnations. They protect you when you are in danger. They comfort you in times of distress. They guide you when you ask for their help.

They cannot force you to do anything, as they respect the free will of each person, but they do offer loving guidance.

At this time of great change. The Angels have come to help and guide us through our transition. In order for us to become a peaceful and loving planet.

More and more people are opening up to the presence of Angels in their life, and are benefiting greatly from their love, comfort, guidance and wisdom.

Archangels are higher 'ranking' angels, who oversee Guardian Angels, and world matters. They have specified roles/jobs. Here is an example of a few Archangels and the roles they perform. All Angels are beneficial beings of wisdom, purity and light.

Archangel Michael is a protector and remover of negativity and fear.

Archangel Raphael is the healer. Who also deals with travel.

Archangel Chamuel brings peace and helps with healing the heart and promoting loving relationships.

Archangel Azrael, comforts the dying and helps us in times of grief. He also helps us through all transitional phases.

Archangel Ariel is the Angel of nature, animals and strength. She can help us to treat nature with respect, as well as giving us strength to deal with life's challenges when we ask her to.

Archangel Uriel, is the Angel of wisdom, and can impart knowledge to you when you ask for specific information, for example during a job interview or exam. After asking the information will simply pop into your head.

Archangel Gabriel helps with pregnancy, creativity, music, writing and communicating.

Part 1. Channelled help from the Angels.

CHAPTER 1. YOU ARE SAFE, LOVED AND NEVER ALONE.

Take a deep breath... YOU are not alone. Take another deep breath... And now another.... Ask us Angels to be with you now... And we ARE immediately with you, giving you all the love and comfort you need. All the time, and every time!

If you feel scared ask me, Archangel Michael to remove all negativity from your life body and house, and know that you are instantly protected. Say "Please Archangel Michael, be with me now and remove any negativity from me, my body and my house, and from all around me. Please sever any negative cords binding me to anyone or place. Please dear Archangel Michael, remove from me any negative attachments now and forever."

Imagine you are being showered with bright white light from above and know that you are instantly protected. For this is my gift to you all, to know you ARE safe and loved at all times and YOU ARE

NEVER ALONE.

We Angels are not linked to any religion and yet are accessible to all. For humanity is one.

You are all part of the same energy that is in everything. You are all equal. You are all the same. Each and every one of you has access to infinite love and wisdom. Each and every one of you has access to our Angelic love, help and guidance 24/7. Anytime and anywhere we can be with you all simultaneously for we are energy and not bound by time or travel restrictions. We want you to call upon us for help whenever and wherever you need. This is our gift to you all.

If you want to be in the company of others, just ask us Angels to bring friends to you. Do not feel lack in your hearts, feel love in your hearts! Say, "please bring me a friend now, let a neighbour knock or let the phone ring, but please bring me a friend now." Wait and see what miracle will come to you! X

In times of sorrow, when all seems too much to

bear, know that you are never alone and ALWAYS loved. When feeling low please say "I release all anger and all sorrow to you dear Angels, and in doing so I AM divinely guided and protected. I AM safe at all times & I AM loved."

WELCOME TO YOUR NEW MOMENT.

We Angels welcome you to this new moment, where anything is possible for you. As you realise what loving, powerful, wise and pure Souls you are, you shape your future and we want you to enjoy every second! Welcome to this new moment! Welcome to your world.

This moment is precious. Your past was a moment ago, an hour ago, a week ago a year ago or many years ago. We welcome you to the present, for this very second is our gift to you!

Everything that has happened to you before no longer has the power to influence your present. That was the past. This precious moment, NOW, has the power to shape your future, and this moment is ever changing becoming the past, second after second. You have this powerful new moment which is your present now and every second, for it is never too late!

As you learn what amazing beings you are.

As you learn that you are limitless, wise, loving and powerful **now**, the past dissolves.

For every thought and dream and decision you make now, shapes your future.

We welcome you to this new second of possibility and positivity! The tracks have changed, you are now on course for the life you were meant to have. Nothing will ever be the same.

Embrace your new life, your new direction! For you are shaping it now... and as each successive moment occurs you have the chance to shape it in the way that serves your highest good. For each moment is new, so please enjoy your ride and journey along your new path. x

CHAPTER 2. RAISING YOUR VIBRATION.

You may have heard a lot about raising your vibration. This may leave some of you fearful, that your vibration is not high enough to communicate with us Angels.

Know that EVERY ONE of you is capable, at any time, to communicate directly with us. All you need to do is simply start talking to us, immediately, just where you are.

In order to understand our loving positive guidance, (for our guidance is ONLY ever supportive and loving) it is useful to raise your vibration by SIMPLY SAYING "Dear Angels clear me of negativity now and restore me to my true and natural state of love and peace and raise my vibration please."

Know, that the second you have uttered these words it is done. With our Love Your Angels x

CHAPTER 3. YOU HAVE IT ALL THERE.

Everything you need is here for you in this beautiful universe.

Say it now "Everything I need is here for me in this big beautiful universe."

How does that make you feel?

Say it a few times and feel your heart expanding and filling with golden light from above. Feel your heart full of love and hope, knowing that everything is here for you, EVERYTHING YOU NEED. As you feel comfortable and secure, relax knowing all you have to do is ask us Angels, for what you need, whilst feeling that loving heart expanding energy and IT will come.

What you need will come to you when you just ask. Talk to us like we are your best friends, because we are! SMILE WE ARE WITH YOU NOW. X! For the Universe provides everything you need; the air you breathe, the food you eat and those feelings of love, that are within YOU at all times. THOSE FEELINGS OF LOVE COME FROM WITHIN YOU! You are so much more powerful than you know and your love is the key. Your love, frees you from all boundaries.

You were born pure. Your heart is pure love! In split second you can choose a different life, a happier life.

Call on us Angels, we can only help you, when YOU ask us to remove your fears and doubts. Feel full of love! Now imagine yourself being showered with white sparkling light from above, pouring over you and into you and filling you up! Now see that white light turn golden. Feel that golden light within you and around you and know you are safe. Now and Forever. X

CHAPTER 4. CHANNELLING.

It is easy for you to channel your own messages from the Angels. You do not need special training, or to pay someone else to do it for you. It is instant and effective.

Just get a pen and paper or open a blank document on your device. It IS however important for you to save it, for when you read back over your channelled messages you will be amazed at the amount of loving guidance you have received this year, this week or just today. ☺

Yes! We Angels tell you to smile a lot. A tendency to get too serious all the time takes the joy out of life, then you wonder why you are surrounded by so much dense heavy energy.

Please ask Archangel Michael to clear your space of dense energy, but ALSO remember to SMILE as this raises YOUR VIBRATION. Also when you smile, by the law of attraction, you will smile more, the law of attraction multiplies what you feel and think and brings it to you.

So when you smile, cosmically you are putting more 'smiles' in your shopping cart and those smiles will come to you with good and happy reasons for expressing them!

Now, with your pen and paper or word doc, write, "Please dear Angels help me." (We Angels work on free will, yours that is and we will not intervene in your life without your request.)

So write, "Please Angels help me" and then write your question anything from the mundane to the all encompassing.

Then, simply write the answer that comes to you. The answer WE channel to you.

Do not over think it. Just write.

You can keep going for as long or as short as you like.

You will be amazed at the help that comes.

Our messages are ONLY ever loving and helpful. If you feel scared, because you have been taught that only crazy people hear messages, (technically you won't hear them as such, you will just know them) if you feel scared at any time for any reason.

Just ask, "Archangel Michael please be with me now and remove any negativity and negative attachments".

Feel yourself being showered with white light and KNOW THE SECOND YOU ASK FOR PROTECTION IT IS THERE! DONE!

Whilst you and your mind, adjusts to the fact that you are not alone and continually supported by US, The Angels and a Universe that loves and supports you. You may well want to ask for this.

There really is nothing to fear, but fear itself and that is only produced by your ego mind and IT IS NOT REAL! You truly are supported and loved by

US all of the time. You need not feel lonely because all you have to do is ask and we are immediately with you. ☺ X So Smile!

CHAPTER 5. MANIFESTING & THE LAW OF ATTRACTION.

Most of your life is governed by the law of attraction. This is not just the trendy phrase of the moment, informing you on how to manifest the life you want. It is basic Physics too. Where you put your attention is what you attract.

So if you want to be happy, you have to think yourself happy. Think happy thoughts, even if you do not feel happy now. When you feel unhappy, you manifest more unhappiness. Think what it would feel like to be happy! Imagine being happy.

What would that feel like?

Think yourself into being happy! Whilst you think these new happy thoughts feel it too. FEEL what you would feel like if you were happy. Your THOUGHTS combined with your FEELINGS are what manifest your life.

So it is vital to think how you WANT to feel, instead

of what you do not want to feel. The law of attraction will bring you what you think.

It is vital to only think yourself into the solution NOT think about the problem. With practise you will see your life improve rapidly. The more you focus on what YOU WANT, as opposed to what you don't, the more RAPIDLY results will appear. This is our gift to you, the secret to manifesting the life you want! Enjoy it now and every day. x

It is all up to you!

You are made out of the same energy that created this world and everything in it.

Everything is made up of the same energy! We keep telling you, that YOU are so much more powerful than you know. Every bit of your life can be changed by changing your thoughts. Never forget; the energy that you are is the same energy that is in every living thing. The same energy that is us, the Angels. We are just without physical form. We can be everywhere at once.

WE are not limited by time or space. Yet we are made of the same energy. This sacred energy is you too! YOU have physical form, but you are made of the same PURE sacred energy! Physical & Human you may be, but you are a spiritual being, living a human existence, not a human being living a spiritual existence.

When you realise this, you will treat each other with the love and reverence you so deserve.

We come to guide you at this time in your evolution, to remind you of this..,. YOU ARE pure love; you are PERFECT just as you are.

When you release your fear to us simply by saying Angels take my fear now please, you will become a peaceful and loving planet.

It starts with YOU. Don't get sidetracked into worrying how all this fits in with your neighbours or others in the world.

We guarantee you, there are far more of you out

there who want to reconnect with your power and what pure and loving beings that you really are, than those that don't.

This is why we have answered so many of your calls for help and peace, by sending you these messages, to help you all lead a beautiful life, which is your destiny!

Do not let media and films scare you into believing in doom and gloom. You are, ALL, RECONNECTING WITH YOUR true power at this time. YOU ARE ALL, RECONNECTING TO WHAT YOU REALLY ARE, AND THAT IS BEINGS OF TOTAL LIGHT AND IMMENSE LOVE. Step forward into your new life for we love you very much! X

40

CHAPTER 6. HEALING.

We are glad that so many of you are seeking out alternative healing to complement modern medicine.

Reiki, Massage and Angel healing are becoming more popular, as humanity evolves into remembering that we are made up of pure energy and it is blockages in this energy that cause many illnesses. For instance Angel Healing is a method of channelling higher source healing energy from, for example, Archangel Raphael through one person, normally the healer into another person, normally the recipient.

We Angels want you to know that YOU all can be the conduit for healing YOURSELF, without the need for a healer.

Yes sometimes it's nice to go to someone and pay to have them perform this service for you, because they have been doing it for a while and are practised at it, but we have to let you know, that you are all capable of doing this for yourself. YOU are all capable of channelling healing direct from source into your own body, the body of a loved one, or a pet.

So let's go... Start By Saying "Archangel Michael please protect me whilst I am doing this healing and let only good pass through me, and into me" Then say "Archangel Raphael please be with me now and channel your healing into me".

Imagine Archangel Raphael's green healing light passing through you from high up above, down through your head, into your body and out through your hands, into the part you want to heal. If you feel guided to move your hands around to other parts do so. You need not touch the part; you can do it just by placing your hands above the area.

When you feel compelled to stop, that is the session finished. Then, imagine yourself and the recipient of the healing being showered with white light from above, place your feet on the ground and the feet of the recipient, and imagine you are both separately anchored to the ground by golden roots from each of your feet. This is called grounding and it reconnects you to the earth. Drink some water too.

Explain to the recipient of the healing, that you both are visualising a shower of golden light going through you from above and that their 'golden roots' are grounding them to this earth.

How did you feel? Did you feel tingling, warmth or cold anywhere? Did the recipient? All this is positive and shows the healing was working. Wasn't that easy and fun? We hope you like our gift of healing for you. It can remove pain too. You cannot overdose on this type of pure healing. Healing will balance you when you need it, even if you need it daily. X

CHAPTER 7. ADDICTION.

Addiction to anything, whether it be food, alcohol, sex, drugs or anything taken to excess, to enhance feelings of well-being is a cry for your Soul to be acknowledged. The higher part of your being is known as your soul. It is pure energy, meaning it is pure and it is energy. Therefore, it is pure energy in its highest form.

Your soul knows only love and perfection and happiness and it remembers this from incarnation to incarnation. You are re-born into this world all knowing and this precious knowledge that you are born perfect, just as you are, that you are born with unlimited love just as you are, and that you are pure just as you are is a constant source of trauma within you.

On the one hand you **know** this to be true. Yet as you move through life, you let other people influence the way you feel, and slowly but surely you let yourself be convinced by others that you are not perfect, don't have perfect love within you and are not pure, just as you are.

You therefore go through life, trying to reproduce the feelings that you know are rightfully your natural state of being. You try desperately to reproduce feelings of total peace, total love and total joy within you.

You have found that your addiction brings a similar feeling to you, so your addiction increases. But these feelings that you are producing within your body and mind are **poor reproductions**, so it continues.

Your soul is literally crying out to be acknowledged and once you acknowledge your beautiful soul, you are on the first step to total joy, total peace and total happiness.

This will happen the minute you connect with your soul. The minute you connect with your soul (the part of you that is eternal and reincarnates) which you can focus on as a bright sparking energy just above your head, connected to you by a silver thread.

You become aware of something more. That YOU

are some thing more! It is pretty instant, but the results will last beyond this recognition of who and what you really are, which is more magnificent than you currently remember!

You are limitless. There is nothing you cannot do, nothing you cannot be and you are a fountain of endless love.

Once you have acknowledged your soul you can ask us Angels to purify and repair it for you. Say "Please Archangel Michael purify and repair my soul for me now." And KNOW that it is done the minute you have uttered these words. Imagine a beam of white light from above purifying and making your soul glow brighter and become whole. Now ask Archangel Michael, "Please vacuum any negativity from me, and sever any cords of negativity to or, from anyone or any place.

And please remove from me now, any need in me for anything that is not for my best and highest good ".

Now say, "I Release to you NOW Angels, my need

for my addictions." Imagine yourself being showered with pure white light from above; imagine it in every cell of your body, every muscle, every fibre of your being and all around you, protecting you with a white force-field of protection and positivity.

This you can do as much as you like, you CAN do this every day if you wish.

You can do it as many times a day as you wish.

Know us Angels only want the best for you and we are here with you the second you ask us to be.

We are without physical form and we can be everywhere at once.

There is no correct time to talk to us; you can talk to us as much as you wish.

There is no right or wrong way to talk to us. You

don't need clean underpants to talk to us.

You don't need to be in a sacred building to contact us.

We are with you at all times. If you wonder why we have not helped you before it is that you have to continuously ask us for help.

We work on the principle of free will, YOURS, we will not interfere in your life unless you ask us to.

Sometimes we guide you to your good when you ask, then you choose to go down a different path and this we allow, because we do not judge you ever and YOU HAVE FREE WILL, which we respect. X.

You have to continuously ASK us for help if you want help. The sooner you realise you can contact us regularly by talking to us, the sooner you will see great improvements happen, as if by miracle in your life. X

The second you connect with your Soul and realise how wonderful, pure loving and perfect you are, feelings of extreme joy and well-being and happiness will be with you.

The more you acknowledge your true essence, the more joy you will know. The more joy, everyone knows, the happier everyone will be and your Planet will not need war, hatred and negativity.

Once YOU all reconnect with who you are, the perfect, unlimited beings which you are, all will change in YOUR world for the better. This WE promise you! X

CHAPTER 8. TIME FOR YOU.

In this fast paced busy world it is essential for you to take time out for yourself. Quiet time away from the TV and media devices is vital for your well-being. Sleep in a room without media devices in them. They emit energy frequencies that are not compatible with your body being able to get into a state of total rest.

All this input from other sources, stops you looking within and hearing the truth. You have all the answers within you. You just need quiet time for reflection. We know some of you fill your world with constant noise whether it is from radio, television or computers and there is nothing wrong with absorbing entertainment in this way, but balance and quiet time for reflection, are needed.

As you start to make a programme to include quiet time in your life, you will feel comforted as opposed to lonely. Your brain will produce self soothing frequencies that will allow you to connect to your joy. Answers to your questions will come to you as if by magic.

At first you may be fearful of having quiet time, you may even feel guilty for turning off your phone. Feelings of unease are there, to show you something needs to change in your world.

Feelings of unease are **not good**. Feelings of comfort **are good**.

When you feel unease with anything or anyone, your intuition is alerting you to change the situation you are currently in.

YOU crave quiet time. YOU need quiet time. Your soul needs this time away, to help you discover what you want and where you want to be. It is reboot time for your mind and body. It is all about balance in life. We are not telling you to become a hermit, but quality, quiet time for yourself, is vital for your well-being.

If you feel that too much time spent in reflection will alert you to things that are wrong with your life, then that is exactly why you need this time.

Any discomfort you experience will be short lived.

Any discomfort you feel is a way of your higher self, your soul, alerting you to facts and situations in your life that you are not happy with. Realising that there are aspects in your life that you are not happy with, is the first step to understanding <u>what</u> you need to change in your life to ensure that you <u>are</u> happy!

You may feel there are only a few changes which need to be made in your life and, these you will find easy to make.

Some of you may find there are many changes you wish to make to your life and to ensure you are at the happiest you can be.

Finding true happiness in your life is one of the most important tasks you will ever do. Finding happiness in your life is a more important task than your work or money. When you start to break down what you want in life, start by asking yourself, "If money was no object what would I love to do… or be...or where would I love to live"?

You may think jetting about with a celebrity lifestyle is what you hanker after, but it is often only the means to an end.

As you delve deeper, you will find that it is freedom, love, joy and enthusiasm, which you want in your life and that actually has nothing to do with money making you happy.

You can have all the money in the world and still be unhappy, if you are not connected to your soul.

Connection to your soul is what makes you happy, as your soul is pure happiness, pure joy and pure love. When you have quiet time you connect to your soul, your soul will show you what you need to change in order to be happy. We the Angels want every single person to live in a state of happiness and joy. It is your right to live in a state of happiness and joy.

Many of our Earthly friends have realised that many changes are required for them to get from where they are, to where they want to be and they are scared of this change.

Know that there is nothing to be scared of, even if suddenly your whole life needs a shake up and your whole life needs to change.

This will happen and it will happen easily.

Ask us Angels, "Angels please remove my fear now and guide me to find and make the changes that will bring me true happiness". KNOW THE SECOND YOU ASK IT IS DONE!

You don't need to worry about leaving your job or changing your life. You don't need to worry about money or how this will all occur. It matters how you ask us though. Don't put emphasis on what you do not want, simply ask us to help you. We will guide you to the best solutions for you, easily, as if by magic.

All you need to do is ask us for help and guidance and to make your transition smooth.

All you need to ask us is "Please Dear Angels, help me to live a happy life. Guide me to my highest and best good, now please. Remove from me, limitations placed on me, by myself & others.

Guide me to accept the help and good now. Help me to live the life I was meant to, now!

Please help me Dear Angels to make my transition smooth".

Imagine yourself being showered with golden light from above, cleansing every cell, every part of your mind, shattering your old worn out thought patterns.

Imagine this gold light protecting you. Imagine this gold light in you, and in every cell brightening you from within and forming a protective bubble around you.

Ask us this, as many times as you need. Even if it is many times in the day.

Keep a notebook/journal, the minute you start. Record how your life is.

Record what happens next.

We the Angels know that our earthly friends have a tendency not to focus on the good that happens in their life, as it happens.

We want to bring your attention to the great changes that are happening in your life, from the first small amounts of good, which we are helping you to manifest, to the huge moments of wonder that starts to happen in your life, those that make you sing for joy.

By keeping a journal you will notice the good as it is happening.

As we have explained in the section on manifesting the life you want, concentrating on how your life is and the things that are wrong, will only manifest more wrong. By asking us for your highest good, we are taking that entire burden from you and allowing you to receive the life and happiness you want. The life and happiness that is yours!

Yes, we expect you to go to job interviews that are sent your way. We want you to visit the new homes you ask us for, those which we place in your path.

We really want you to take a chance on love, when we send your special soul mates to you. "How will I know these are the right things for me? " You ask.

If you feel a sick feeling in your tummy or any form of worry, it is not right for you! If you feel good, it is good! Simple! You have been fitted with a gut feeling for a reason. Your gut feeling is your GPS system to help you navigate your way in life. If however, you are unsure whether it is the right direction for you, ask us!

Then say:-

"Please Archangel Michael remove from me any negativity and negative attachments now". Imagine yourself showered with white light from above, imagine it in every part of you. Imagine it in every cell.

Imagine it all around you. Imagine yourself glowing with white bright light, that turns gold, & know you have been protected and then ask again "Please Angels guide me to my highest good now!" You can also ask "Is this for my highest good now?"

If you feel a deep knowing that it is, proceed! If you feel doubt or fear, know that it is not the way to proceed.

Trust us, and trust your gut feeling. Your gut feeling and Us the Angels are there to help you navigate your way through your life. With our love. May you all experience the perfect lives that you were meant to live. X

CHAPTER 9. YOUR EMPOWERMENT.

So many of you think your quest or mission is to save someone else, whether it is a partner or parent, your child or your friend.

Sometimes it is easier for you to place your attention on another. This takes away the focus on yourself.

Sometimes this focus on yourself and your life makes you feel uncomfortable. You are uncomfortable because you cannot immediately see which changes you need to make in your life.

Sometimes you are overwhelmed by your life. You can however see what changes you THINK others should make. It is easier for you to see this, because you have a certain amount of distance from them, which gives you a different perspective on their life as opposed to the perspective you currently have on yours.

It is the difference between viewing your life as

objectively rather than subjectively

We ask you to kindly try to distance your perspective on your own life. For instance, look on your own life as though it was the life of a dearest friend, whom you love very much. (At this point, we remind you that you should value and treat yourself as your dearest friend every single day.)

What advice would you give them? See if you find comfort in this advice, as it applies to your own life.

Be your own guide, that way if you like what advice you give yourself, you can adapt or change the situation so that you have a happier life. If you do not like your own advice you can write it in your journal to look back on later to see if it serves you then.

Always remember though when seeking your own advice ask yourself the one main question "Does this serve my highest good or does this take me further from my highest good?"

If you are true and honest with yourself you will instinctively know in your body, heart and gut, whether this is the correct choice for you. Your body produces feelings of 'good' 'happiness' and 'well-being' if something is right for you. Your body will produce feelings of panic and unease and discomfort, if something is wrong for you.

So many people you know have an opinion on how you should live your life. They may voice their opinions to you freely. They may say they love you and are concerned for your well-being, but ONLY YOU know what you need. This may even upset your loved ones, as it is not what **they** want for you.

What matters is what **you** want, for **you!**

Always aim higher. Always let your spirit soar.

Dream big and the Universe will support you.

Dream small and all you will know, is a smaller life than the one you deserve.

Please know that your soul is a highly evolved energy, which knows only love and peace and good. Learn to trust your own soul's guidance.

In life, there is only one law, do what you will, as long as it does not harm or interfere with another. That pretty much covers all situations, but also know you are a pure being, of only good and when you align with this truth, good will enter all aspects of your life.

If you are confused or overwhelmed or scared, ask Us Angels to help you, by simply saying:

"Please dear Angels, guide me to my highest good. Show me how to make changes in my life and send me the guidance I need to move toward a happier life." Imagine white light showering you from above, filling you, surrounding you, and protecting you. Know that the minute you ask us it is done.

So many times you ask for what you **think** you need, rather than asking for **the guidance to know what you need.**

We will not interfere in your life, as we say so many times YOU have free will which we respect. But know dear soul that it is your divine right to lead a happy life and you only have to ask us to intervene and help you. For we love you and want you to have the very best life.

Know this, it is your ONLY quest, to save yourself and make yourself whole. By doing this you will have a better life and inspire others to make changes, so that they have better lives too.

Never try to impose your ideas and wishes on another. What is right for you, is only right for you! You can never know what is right for someone else. Just like we (The Angels) give you free will to choose your path you have to honour every other human in this way too. You have to honour the free will of every other human being, whether it is your child, friend, or love partner.

We advise you of this because the reason your world has problems, is because each person thinks he or she knows how another should live.

Friends, family and religions, constantly bombard you with information telling you how to live.

This way is not of use to you beautiful souls any more.

So much war has been committed by one group of people, telling another group of people how to live. Religions commit this crime regularly. You are ALL EQUAL, you are all the same energy. You ALL have the same feelings.

YOU ALL want love, security, happiness, freedom, health and joy. It is time for you to honour the divine presence in each other. Every one of you is a sacred & pure being. You are ALL powerful. You are ALL pure. You are ALL wise. YOU are all full of immense love. You, each and every one of you, knows the way to treat each other.

You all know that you do not want to be judged for your choices. You all know that you do not want to be hurt, humiliated, criticised, bullied, have your freedom taken from you... You all know you want to feel safe.

So the only way to treat each other is how you wish to be treated at your highest ideal. You are all one and you are all the same. In order to connect spiritually to each other you need to stop criticising each other and each others religious beliefs. YOU ARE ALL PERFECT and this you know to be the truth in your heart. So please dear Souls, stop hurting each other and start loving each other. X

CHAPTER 10. LOVE.

Love is your most powerful tool as it soothes everything, heals everything and transcends time and space. Are you not capable of loving those who are no longer here as much as you did when they were here?

All you have to do is be open to love, time and time again, as love is the greatest, purest energy there is. Do not ever forget that! You have an endless amount of love within you. If you feel a need to clear your heart of previous pain - ask us!

Say, "Dear Archangel Chamuel, heal my heart of past pain please and help me to open my heart to pure love again." Imagine a golden light filling your heart and then imagine pink rays, radiating out from your heart into the world, touching everything. These pink rays will shine back to you too, sending love everywhere and as you are part of everything, you too will receive this perfect love.

Forgive all those who you perceive have hurt you.

Often, what you perceive as hurt is just an individual exercising their free will. If a partner wishes to leave a relationship, it is their choice to exercise their free will.

It really does not have anything to do with you. Meaning it is not about who or how you are. It is one soul moving in a direction that they choose to, out of their free will.

Too many times humans see love as ownership of another.

Each human has a pure and wonderful soul, which is full of love and just because their life takes them in a different direction it really should not hurt you.

Yet it does and the way to minimise this hurt is to bless everyone for their choices.

When looking for a love partner, instead of setting your heart on a particular person and trying to mould them to how you want them to be, accept that each individual is exactly that, INDIVIDUAL.

Honour time spent with a partner. If you were both happy, be glad that you got to spend a portion of your life sharing love and the journey of life together.

If your journey together lasts for a long and happy time, then honour that and give thanks for it.

If your time together ends, think instead how wonderful it was, that you spent the time you had together, rather than wishing it was still the same.

Know that to move on and grow and learn, is nothing to be scared of. You are always safe.

In this world of constant change, it is not surprising that people change too.

Things that interested you as a child no longer interest you. Food that you once loved to eat, no longer holds the same appeal. Yet you expect your relationships to defy change.

We want you, ALL to be happy. We want you all to love because love is the greatest, purest, energy there is.

There is one thing to remember though. When YOU love, those feelings of love and adoration for your partner come from your own heart!

Those feelings of love are yours alone! There is nothing to stop you from feeling that love, everyday, with or without a partner. You can have those wonderful overwhelming feelings of love, for yourself, your pets, your friends, and your fellow human beings.

Love is not a condition of being in a relationship. LOVE IS WITHIN YOU AT ALL TIMES.

Now, we know that you want to share a loving relationship, so instead of placing your intention on one particular person try saying

"Please dear Angels; bring to me a loving partner that will be for my and their highest good."

And see what happens, but remember a partner cannot provide for you something that you cannot give to yourself. You have to love yourself and be emotionally full, in order to attract a partner who will love you in the way you wish to be loved.

There is no point expecting someone to give you something that is not in your own heart for yourself.

When we talked earlier about manifesting the life you want, the law of attraction will only bring to you more of what you have, so if you don't trust, you will attract a partner who doesn't trust.

If you don't love yourself and realise just how wonderful you are, you will not attract a partner who thinks you are wonderful.

It all starts with your inward feeling. What you radiate out will come back to you, it is the law of attraction.

The only way **not** to have love in your life is to not give love. The more love you give the more love you will attract!

This love is good for you to pour into the world as a whole, but remember in terms of private relationships, love should be easy and feel good.

Trust your emotion to alert you, when you are in a one-sided relationship. All pure love should feel good and easy. If you have to force yourself to be with a person, then the relationship is not for you.

Always honour and follow the guidance of your

own heart and intuition. You are fitted with emotion responses, to guide you through life. Always remember if it feels good it is. If it feels not good, your body will produce feelings of unease to guide you. Trust yourself. Never be in a relationship that is not for your highest good.

I repeat to you, dear Soul, if you wish to heal your heart please ask us to help you, and Say:

"Dear Archangel Chamuel heal my heart of past pain please and help me to open my heart to pure love again." Imagine a golden light filling your heart and then imagine pink rays radiating out from your heart, into the world, touching everything.

These pink rays will shine back to you too, sending love everywhere and as you are part of everything, you will receive this perfect love too. With our love. X

CHAPTER 11. FEAR & WORRY.

Most of your problems stem from fear and worry. Fear and worry are not emotions, they are thoughts.

Thoughts produce an emotion in your body but thoughts themselves can be changed quickly. Try thinking of a sunny day on the beach, now think of a cat.

How quickly did your thoughts change?

Yes! Wasn't that immediate? ☺ (Please smile! You are doing well and learning new ways to live. Is that not reason to smile?)

Once you change your thought the emotion changes.

Whatever the problem you are facing, you will be able to deal with it more effectively if you can think clearly, without the all-encompassing fear and panic, flooding your body.

So if you are in a state of panic, worry or fear, say "I release my fear to you now Angels. Take my fear now please."

Notice how your feelings have changed, you are now aware of a sense of relief. Try saying it a few times more.

Then say, "Please dear Angels guide me to a fast solution to my problem please and protect me from harm now." Imagine white light around you and in you, and know that we are with you and assisting you, the second you ask us.

The human race has seen so much suffering and hardship and in these times of easy mass media, you are constantly bombarded with images that make you afraid and worried.

On the one hand, to have access to what is going on in the world is a good thing, as you are no longer being kept in the dark about what happens in your world. However this has led you to be in a constant state of fear and worry.

We Angels advise you not to watch the news before bedtime so that you are not taking these images with you into your dream and rest time.

As we have explained, the Law of Attraction manifests into your life what you think about and where you place your attention, manifests that into your life. So lengthy exposure of your mind, thoughts and feelings to these troubles and worry, only produce more trouble and worry, not just in your world, but in the world as a whole.

What will help you is to only concentrate on the SOLUTION rather than the problem. We are not telling you to avoid being aware of others conflict, but to imagine them all happy and peaceful. Imagine them all loving each other healed and safe. Imagine this with love and focus. That, according to the Law of Attraction, will produce the **solution** to the problem by making you aware of how powerful each and every one of you beautiful souls are.

Then **you** will become not only the hero in your own life, but the hero the world needs. Do not worry what others are doing, or thinking. As we constantly tell you, it starts with YOU!

YOU have the power to make the changes that you want to see in the world. The Law of Attraction is your tool, to enable you to have the life you want. The law of Attraction is the tool in which to bring about the changes this beautiful world of yours needs. Remember the law of attraction works by THOUGHT/INTENTION + FEELING = RESULTS.

The results happen faster than you can imagine!

Your imagination is limited by what you have come to know. Your imagination is in fact, as huge and vast as the universe and beyond.

You are powerful energy, you are pure, wise energy, and everything and everyone, is made up of this timeless, endless, pure energy. You are without limit. It is time to realise your own power and imagination, is pure and limitless.

The Law of attraction works on attracting more of the same, so it is essential for you to only call to you the things you wish for, to only call to you positive things for your greater good.

So Dear souls focus on Love. Happiness. Healing. Harmony. Kindness. Compassion. Abundance and Health. Basically only focus your thoughts and wishes for the world, and each person on it, to receive their highest and best life possible.

If you start bringing in greed, selfish motives anger, fear and hate, you will not only manifest that for the world, but you will attract more of that into your own lives, as you have seen happen already.

If you are fearful of bringing more of this into your own life, ask us Angels to remove your fear.

Say, "Please dear Angels remove my fear and worry now! Please restore me to my highest self, a being of pure and wise love. Guide me to my highest good."

Then imagine yourself showered with white light, surrounding you and going into each cell of your body. Feel yourself become transformed from a panic state, to a calm state. Feel how instantly you feel better and at peace. This you can do as much as you like, as often as you like. You will not tire us or bore us. We are here for each and every one of you 24/7 and WE want you all to have the love, peace, happiness and security, which are rightfully yours. X ☺

We talked about Global fear and worry. Now let us bring our attention to personal fear and worry.

We know many of you wake in the middle of the night with your fears and worries. We know, money worries, trouble you.

We ask you to only concentrate on the solution, not the worry.

So if its money you need to pay your bills only concentrate on the amount you need. Do not focus on the how or why.

When you think of the how or why, you limit the good we have for you.

Your limited thoughts can only produce more of what you know. We however have a vast concept of abundance and can bring you things, far greater than you, in your current state can dream of. When you only keep thinking of the **solution**, not the problem, you access this greatness.

One of our earthly friends was so worried about her bills, and never having enough, all she manifested into her life by the Law of Attraction were more bills and not having enough.

We taught her that her bills are good. It is a way of proving she was circulating the energy of money well. The bigger her bills meant, that by the law of attraction the more money would come to her. Yet all she focused on was the lack, and not having enough, so as she earned more, she still never had more!

The law of attraction continued to bring her exactly what she thought about, - remember, THOUGHT +

FEELING (EMOTION) = RESULTS. She thought lack therefore she manifested more lack.

We showed her to concentrate on the solution.

At first, she was in such a panic state, she thought of a poor solution, a loan, this was manifested quickly as her intention and thought was strong.

She received the loan and is still paying it off 3 years later. We have shown her that wasn't really a solution. The solution would have been to think of the money needed and concentrate on **that amount coming,** and the bill getting paid instead of a loan!

This is what happens, when you think about 'the how' and 'the why', your limitations can only bring to you what you can conceive based on past experiences.

We want you to open up to the vastness of your potential. The vastness and limitless of what you are. What you are capable of achieving. What you are capable of imagining.

So her real solution was to think about the sum needed, to ONLY think about the sum coming to her and think how good it feels to actually pay the bill. To see herself paying the bill immediately, not delaying it or putting it off for some future time, where worry and fear would torment her, but to think and feel of actually having the money and paying the bill **now**.

Intending to pay that bill now, for intent is a powerful tool in aiding manifestation of your goal.

At first her fear got worse because she berated herself for not being able to change her thought patterns quickly enough. We Angels channelled information to her, to be kinder to herself, and praise herself for the positive changes she was making in her thought process.

We showed her, that taking responsibility for her thought process was nothing to fear. We showed her, that thinking of the **solution** actually works.

Sometimes though, her mind wanted to go back to thinking it was impossible for her to get that large, amount in her time-frame.

We showed her that her pre-conceived ideas were actually stopping her progress.

We kept telling her that she, like every other being was pure, wise and powerful, and that her way forward, was to stop thinking she was, in any way limited, in a limited world. We showed her, she was an unlimited being in an unlimited universe and the only thing holding her back was herself and her pre-conceive ideas.

Like YOU, she learned that she was a pure, wise, powerful & loving energy (her Soul) and that she was letting her lowest self, the ego, torment her with thoughts of lack.

N.B The ego is not as you have perhaps always understood. Ego is the lower human self that fills you with fear, hate and panic and can be silenced the second you realise your soul is pure, wise and powerful. That is the essence of your being.

Once you acknowledge the energy within you, that reincarnates from lifetime to lifetime, the energy in you is your SOUL. Once you align with the fact that YOU have a soul and it is pure, powerful, loving and perfect.

Once you align with the truth, that YOU ARE PURE AND POWERFUL AND LOVING AND PERFECT, then you will lose your fear and worry.

As she started to learn this and focus on the **solutions** to her problems, **not** the problems themselves, she started to feel JOY.

This by the law of attraction brought her more joy.

She knew that she needed help in overcoming her worry and fear, and continued to ask us "Please dear Angels remove my fear and worry now. Restore me to my highest self. A being of pure and wise love. Guide me to my highest good."

Changes started happening quickly and with her concentration, she managed to pay her huge bill in two weeks! She is writing this, as she has asked us to channel this help to you, as we have channelled the help to her.

She wants **you** to experience the wonder that she has experienced, by inviting US, the Angels, into your life for guidance and connecting you to the intelligence and pure love and power that we all have within us - namely your soul.

So whatever your fear or worry is, please Dear Soul, do NOT concentrate on the problem ONLY **the solution**.

If you are in a panic state, ask us to help you to find the solution, in order for you to concentrate on manifesting every solution to every problem you have.

Once you find solutions to your problems, you will see them as challenges, that are easily surmountable and then you will be able to live the lives of happiness that are rightfully yours.

CHAPTER 12. Illness.

Most illness is caused by blocks in your energy field. The energy gets stuck and does not flow properly. Illness can occur through thought patterns too. Just as we have said before, what you think becomes your reality.

By the law of attraction, what you think, brings more of the same.

There is no good you thinking I want to be well, as what you are thinking is lack of 'well'. This only attracts more lack of being well.

We know dear Soul, that when you are unwell, it is hard to focus on feeling well but that will bring you more WELL!

Thinking I AM WELL AND FIT AND HEALTHY, will bring you more WELL and FIT and HEALTHY.

We understand that this concept may be strange for you but dear Soul, think of those people in the world who have healed themselves of terminal illness.

Some people call this a miracle, but miracles happen every second of every day, everywhere.

Just look at how each blade of grass knows to reach for the sun. Notice the miracle that is you and all the amazing things that you do without even being aware.

You are doing it, now - breathing, reading, drinking or eating something, and all this, you do at the same time, ☺ yet you do not think of this as a miracle. Well dear Soul, are these things not miracles?

Of course they ARE!

The fact is you are accustomed to them and you have stopped seeing them as miracles. We Angels want you to experience even more wonderful miracles in your lives.

So please start expecting more miracles and notice them when they arrive!

You are a miracle! There is no difference between from the people who have cured themselves of illness and YOU. Simply the thought process

As we have said before, THINK ONLY OF THE SOLUTION, NOT the problem, to attract more of the same. By the law of attraction, what you think brings more of the same.

So please dear Soul, think of the solution. How would it feel to be well?

How good would that feel?

Keep thinking **that** and only **that!**

Please Dear Soul, when improvements occur, do not dismiss them. Notice **any** and **every** improvement, no matter how small and say it out loud!

Say, "Every cell in my body knows how to heal itself and I AM getting better!"

"I feel stronger and healthier than I have ever done before and it's great!"

As you say this, imagine golden light from above showering you and going into each cell. Imagine each cell vibrating with health, and continue to say, "I AM improving, that's great! My health is improving. I AM getting better each day!

Every cell in my body knows how to heal itself and I AM getting better!

I feel stronger and healthier than I have ever done before, and it's great!"

Feel the golden light in you and around you, in each cell and know that we, the Angels, are helping your body to heal itself.

We have come to teach you what miracles you are, and what miracles you can achieve. We love you and you are safe! X ☺ S.M.I.L.E!

CHAPTER 13. GOALS & DREAMS

So many of you believe it is wrong to have goals and dreams. So many of you have seen people in power, abuse their power and it has made you fearful of embracing your goals and dreams and making them happen.

So many of you think there is no point in even having a goal or a dream in the first place.

Know this, it is your right to dream and aspire.

You have been given goals and dreams for a reason! The reason is to improve your lives. Once you achieve your goals and dreams, you will inspire others to do so too. You will show them that they can dream, have goals and make their own dreams come true.

You will be an inspiration to others, to better their own lives, as you better your own life.

Please be willing to share your stories of achievement with others.

As the world's energy rises, in a positive direction, people will be inspired by you, rather than jealous of you.

Once you show each other, you can **all** achieve your dreams and goals, each and every one of you, will know there is no cause to be jealous. You are **all** powerful and wise and you can **all** achieve now.

There is everything that you need that you could wish for right now, here in this world!

It is simply a case of calling it to you, by imagining the dream, focusing on it and bringing it into your realm.

If you want change yet are unsure of what to wish or dream for, ask US Angels. Say,

"Please guide me to goals and dreams that are for my highest and best good. Please help me to soar now." Know that we will not guide you to anything that is not in yours or the world's highest good.

Know, that what we can guide you to is so much greater than anything you can wish for yourself.

We inspire you to reach for your own goals and dreams. For once the world's inhabitants know that they are pure and loving souls and their wishes can be fulfilled. You will be so excited that your dreams are coming to fruition. You will be excited too, about helping those less fortunate to accomplish their goals. Good, manifests more good, by The Law of Attraction.

You have seen in the last 30 years, a rise in Global help. That help is possible because of YOU, not organisations or Governments but YOU!

YOU, each and every one of you, are the beautiful souls who help each other either through monetary gifts to charities or directly to areas in need. This you do frequently and with love.

You ARE the caring, loving souls!

This is our proof to you, that you are those loving, pure and capable souls of which we constantly remind you! x

We have noticed that many of you think there is merit in struggle.

The words you use for instance, 'struggling artist', 'no gain without pain' or 'I'd rather be nice than rich'.

These are insane limitations, which you have placed upon yourselves. YOU have fabricated this law for yourself.

The Universe is vast and abundant and filled with endless possibilities, if only you would open your eyes to your own magnificence.

We urge you to dream and soar and make your life

a better place. By making your life a better place, you will make the world a better place too. You will then inspire others to make their life better. This is a positive circle of good attracting more good.

CHAPTER 14. FREEDOM.

Each and every one of you beautiful souls was born free. The only limitations placed on your freedom, stem from yourself and others.

Like everything else, this can change.

Unfortunately, there are places in the world, where ruling bodies remove an individual's freedom.

Yet their mind, heart and soul is still free, even when physically they may not be free.

We ask that everyone in any situation where their freedom has been taken away, asks US Angels.

"Please Angels, free me from this situation now! Please empower me now! Guide me to free myself from this situation now!

Archangel Michael please protect me now!"

Imagine white light from above showering you and protecting you. Then imagine golden light filling you up, from your head to your feet, in you and around you, going into every cell in your body, giving you extreme power. Empowering you! Giving you the strength and protection that you need.

Ask us Angels "Please be with me now and help me to find the solutions to break free." Know we are instantly with you, loving you, supporting you and helping you.

Know that your solution will reveal itself to you and know that you are safe! Know that we are constantly with your Body and Soul, the second you ask us to be. Know that you are safe, no matter what!

For those of you in 'safe' countries, where the imprisonment of your spirit is caused by obligation to family or friends, understand that this is your moment of freedom, now and forever.

Know that you have the right to freedom and no matter what another wishes for you, that this is **your** life and you were born free, to make your own choices and decisions and to follow your own dreams.

Many of you have been negatively influenced for too long, by parents or friends, who say that they want the best for you.

They believe they know best and are acting out of love, yet they are imposing their wants and desires onto you and your life. These are things that they want and desire for themselves, yet sometimes, out of misguidance they think that you will want those things too.

Know dear Soul that only **you** know what you want and you have to be brave enough to follow your **own** dreams.

When you ask us, we Angels will help you find **your** way. The way that is unique to you.

Forgive those that try to influence you and trust your intuition, that you do know what you want. It is safe for you to be strong, free, powerful and follow your dreams.

We will help you find your dreams and passions and how to live the lives that you were meant to live. We will help you live in total peace and joy. We will help you to live a life without fear. You are not meant to life a life of fear! We Angels have come to answer your cries for help at this time.

You Dear Souls, think it is normal to fear everything. You fear that you cannot be free and follow your dream because it will not fit in with what others have planned for you. You fear that if something goes 'right', then something else will go 'wrong'.

This way of thinking you think is normal.

You do not think it 'normal' for you to all live a wonderful life of freedom, trust, love, and positivity. This is why you are in such turmoil dear Souls.

Your Soul knows that it is free. Your Soul knows that it is pure. Your Soul knows that it is wise and Your Soul knows pure love!

It is time to free yourself dear Soul, from this previous limited way of thinking.

You are meant to live a life of wonder which is full of good. You then will radiate love and good into your world and by the law of attraction, all that good and love will radiate back to you, bringing you comfort, happiness and the freedom that your soul yearns for.

Ask us dear Soul, we can only help you when you ask us. Say, "Please dear Angels guide me to my highest good. Take away my fear and align me with my true self, which is freedom, love and wisdom. Please show me the way to fulfil my life of highest good **now!**"

Imagine yourself showered from above, with white light raining down on you and into you, filling and surrounding you, covering and protecting you.

Know, that we Angels, will never guide you to harm or to harm another. Know, that as beings of light, once you align yourselves with your light, you will automatically be guided to live the most positive and loving life, far beyond your imagination. Please feel safe and enjoy this wonderful life and have FUN with it! X ☺

CHAPTER 15. SECURITY.

It is your right to feel safe and secure. Know all your needs are provided for, when you ask us. We will always find a safe shelter for you, when you ask us to find one for you.

Security comes from within, it is not external as many of you think. Yes it is natural for you to want to be in a lovely house with comforts and a pleasing environment, but real security is a state within.

Once you know that you are loved and supported by us Angels and a universe that has your best interest at heart, you will feel calmer, safer and more relaxed. As you become aware of our loving presence, you will naturally feel secure.☺

When you are in need of feeling secure, ask us Angels for what you need. Say,

"Angels, please find me a safe and secure home, bring me signs and please guide me to a secure place now!" Obviously you will have to go to shelters or estate agents to find your solution, but know that we will place opportunities in your path to help and guide you the second you ask us to.

CHAPTER 16. TRUST.

Trust is simply knowing and expecting the best outcome to occur in any and every situation. Trust is knowing that it will all work out fine in all situations.

Many of you have forgotten what trust really means. You may think that trust is when you love someone and then they break your trust. Firstly, no-one can break your trust, only yourself.

You were born pure, loving, powerful and trusting and this you know to be true, but human nature forgets these most important empowering truths, because you are constantly told you are not all powerful and that it is wrong to be too trusting. In your hearts and in your souls, you know you are pure love, all powerful pure and trusting beings and when you remember who you are, **you** reclaim your true power.

When you love someone and you think that they have broken your trust, it really has nothing to do with trust or you for that matter!

What is happening, is that you expect a person to act in a particular way and when they don't, you feel hurt, let down and betrayed. You think it is an issue of trust, but it is an issue of expectation.

Every person acts in ways that are acceptable to themselves. This can change with circumstances. How someone acts has no bearing on you. It is personal to them. It is their choice as they have free will, as to how they act.

When you take personally, the actions of another, you rob yourself of **your** power because only you can expect yourself to act in a certain way at any given time. Only you know yourself. When you expect another to act in a certain way, you are having an unreal expectation.

Yes! It is a real and valid expectation to expect and hope that others will behave in a way that is decent, but sometimes in certain situations, people lose their way and act impulsively.

Mostly, they are ashamed of themselves when they act in an unacceptable way. They let themselves down by their behaviour, which is unbearable to them.

Often they cannot admit this to themselves, because the pain of doing so is so great. They know in their heart and soul the decent way to act, yet when they act without thought and consideration, they are going against the truth of their very being, which is a soul that is pure, wise, loving, compassionate and kind. This is why their action will cause them even greater pain than it causes you.

You dear Soul, must be responsible for your emotions and thoughts, as blame is a negative emotion that takes away your own power, keeping you stuck in a negative cycle.

To live in your power, you need to align yourself with real TRUST, knowing that whatever outcome occurs will be the very best and that you are safe, protected and guided to your highest good at all times. That is trust.

Other people's choices have nothing to do with trust. You cannot change another person, but you can change how you react to them.

When you realise that it has nothing to do with you, you will understand that people make their own choices and by removing your judgement of them, you free yourself.

You free yourself, not only from negative emotion but also from judgement of others.

We ask you to say:

"Please Angels, remove from me all judgement and expectation of others and restore me to my true self, which is total peace, love, security and trust."

Imagine yourself showered with white light. Imagine it in every cell of your body and all around you and imagine your heart filled with pure pink light, that radiates out from you, surrounding you with love and into your world.

Know that you are restored to love and that no one can take your power from you, for your power lies in the fact that you love and trust and are powerful and complete in that state.

CHAPTER 17. SEX.

So many of you beautiful Souls have allowed your pain, confusion and conflicting emotions, stop you from enjoying a healthy sex life. Part of your journey here on Earth, as a human being, is to integrate your soul with your body in a way that allows you to live a happy and harmonious life.

You are in a physical human body for a reason, to grow and learn and it is a basic human right to enjoy physical pleasure. Your body was made that way. You were given nerve endings and pleasure zones to enhance your physical experience.

So many of you have conflicting religious doctrines, which dictate how you live. We Angels want you to know it is right and normal to celebrate your sexuality and the physical aspect of love.

There is only one law you need to be aware of, the law of free will. That means that if a sexual act is not agreed to by both parties, then it should not be acted out. If both parties are old enough and coherent enough to agree, then it is consentual sex and both parties involved are in agreement what happens. Rape is never right! Abuse is never right! There is no Soul on this earth who does not instinctively know the way to treat another. Your soul is pure love, pure wisdom, pure peace, pure happiness and you were created perfect.

Every individual has the right to honour their own sexuality, as long as it does not harm or interfere with another.

It is time for you beautiful Souls to forgive past pains and reconnect to each other through love. When you act with love, that all encompassing pure love from your heart, you will know purity and joy.

Then you can reconnect to your **own** beauty and sexuality through your **own** sensuality. Sexuality and sensuality starts with you. It is personal and within you. It has nothing to do with another. It is all about how good **you feel** being you.

During the act of loving sex, it is not just a closeness of bodies but a closeness of souls. An harmonious merging of souls that brings you ecstatic joy.

This is the same ecstatic joy as connection to your own soul brings you. Awareness of your soul (the eternal part of you that reincarnates) is the first step to experiencing joyous connection to your self.

Some of you beautiful souls have had this great gift of the purity and pleasure of the human sexual experience taken from you, by rape or abuse. We Angels want you to know that it is safe for you to heal these past traumas and free yourself from anything that has disconnected you from your own pleasure, sacred sexuality and sensuality.

We ask you to say,

"Please Angels take my fear and shame and return me, body and soul, to purity and wholeness. Heal and empower me now, to enjoy all of life's pleasures. Imagine yourself washed by a white light waterfall from above, going into each cell and memory and cleansing you of all past pain, shame and guilt.

See the waterfall turn golden. See the golden light in every cell of your body. See the golden waterfall surrounding your entire body. Feel yourself cleansed, energized and empowered to live a full and pleasurable life. This is our gift to you. A life of joy, for your body and soul! x

CHAPTER 18. Death & Bereavement & Eternity.

We have come to know that you, in your physical human incarnation, fear death because you are afraid that it is the end.

You are distressed because perhaps you didn't get to do all that you wanted to do, or say things to people, that you wished to say.

Please know dear Soul, that by simply being here, you did accomplish your task in this incarnation... and as far as it being the end – fear not, for nothing is ever the end!

Does a piece of wood not turn into ash when burned?

Do leaves not beautifully turn into nourishing compost which eventually becomes wonderful earth, when they leave the tree?

This is applies to you too dear souls. You are one thing – energy, which incarnates into your human self and just like that piece of wood, you change once again into something else. You return to pure energy, to be reincarnated again.

So, actually there is little change in you from lifetime to lifetime. Your physical body may be gone, but you are a beautiful, bright, loving and pure soul – your energy is endless! This is our gift to you at this time, to remind you of that and to enable you to live without fear.

Know too, that those you have loved who no longer live in the physical realm, are **always** with you, for their soul like yours is eternal.

They are always with you. Talk to them and you will feel their answers, as you calm your heart and mind.

Relax and spend quiet moments talking with them and know the energy that was them, namely their soul, can be with you, as they are not bound by human form and our perception of time and space.

Know dear Soul, that you are always safe and always loved, for us Angels and spirit guides are always with you, to comfort and care for you and guide you to a fearless life full of wonder.

Don't wait for it to be too late in this life to celebrate each other and tell those whom you love just how much you love them!

Don't be so afraid, that you cannot celebrate your life and follow your dreams.

Relax and enjoy this journey and live to the best of your ability.

Go with love, for that is what you pure souls are ultimately here to share and teach each other.

There is nothing for you to fear in death.

Before you came into this incarnation, you agreed to the time span that you would return for, in order to share lessons of love and healing with those who you chose to share lessons of love and healing with.

No doubt you will share more lessons again with people you love, as they are your Soul Family. Soul family bonds are eternal too. Soul family are not the same as your physical family, although some of your physical family can be soul family. Your friends too can be soul family.

The universe is in constant change, yet eternal! Just like you!

Be safe! Be free! Be not afraid, for you have been and will always be!

CHAPTER 19. Body/Body Image.

Before mass media, many more of you were happy with your appearance.

In fact many of you did not pay a whole lot of attention to your appearance. On the plus side, men now take more care in making themselves smell nice and look presentable.

At one time they just washed and went! Some of them didn't even wash! (Yes we Angels understand the importance of humour!)

Previously in our history, simply putting food on the table (or cave!) was important. Keeping out hoards of invading warriors, was important.

Yes, it is important that you take care of yourself. Wash, pamper and look after yourself. It is a way of you showing yourself, that you have self-esteem and love yourself. It is personal. It is for you. It is about loving and caring for who **you** are.

Where all this starts to go wrong is when **you** start comparing yourself to others.

YOU are an individual. You are not 'others'. Being an individual is a great and wonderful gift! There is only one of you and you are unique and magnificent, so why would you want to be like any other? It is time to rejoice in your uniqueness.

Notice how mad fashions can be? Those crazy fads. Sure, sometimes you get it right and look good, but most of the fashions that people emulate are crazy.

Think for a moment of all the really bad fashion looks, that were copied by all those beautiful souls, who forgot that they were unique and wanted to look like each other.

Are you made of plastic and produced on a factory conveyor belt? No! You are not. You are all different and wonderful, just as you are. Just like in nature, each leaf, each snowflake is different. Each animal has different markings and that is wonderful. Not something to erase or airbrush or mould into a uniform look.

Think about how some of you now spray yourself orange.

Do you **really** think that it looks good?

Would you all spray yourselves blue?

Blue is not a natural colour for people, neither is orange.

What about the rise in the use of facial filler and botox. Every single user ends up looking like a cat, with the mouth of a fish.

Do you really think that looks good or normal?

Would you grow fur and a tail if every other human did?

Really dear Souls, you are taking this way too far now and you are losing the plot (as you humans would say)

Love yourself. Look after yourself. Eat healthy organic food so that your body is free from chemicals and you feel good. Ditch those sweet fizzy drinks, which contribute to obesity.

Limit the amount of sugar and fat you consume, so that you will feel good, energised and happy, rather than overweight, lethargic and in pain.

Many of the over processed foods that you consume contribute to inflammation of your body which in turn leads to chronic pain.

Exercise, even if only for a little bit.

As little as 15 minutes exercise a day, will make you feel good and it's easy to do. To save money on expensive gym memberships, why not buy your own exercise bike and use a couple of small weights? Do this in your home, whilst you are watching TV, rather than sitting watching TV it will make you feel great!

A little exercise gets rid of most pains. Drink plenty of water rather than those fizzy drinks.

Water gets rid of headaches. Water flushes toxins out of your body. Water makes your skin more radiant.

Eat fresh organic fruit, salads and vegetables.

These foods carry waste products and toxins safely out of your gut. These foods, also remove inflammation from your body and by simply eating fresh organic fruit, salad and vegetables, you will notice your skin looking more radiant, making you even more beautiful! Organic food is produced without the use of toxic chemicals, so why would you choose to fill your body with things that are not good for it?

These are all improvements that will make you feel great rather than spraying your self orange and

making yourself look like a cat, with a fish mouth.
☺

It is insane that you go to consultants who tell you to have these procedures. It is even more insane that you listen to them, then pay them to perform these procedures.

It doesn't matter what other people are doing dear Soul, it matters what **you** are doing.

Just because shops sell food that is over processed and full of chemicals, which make you ill, doesn't mean that **you** have to buy it.

Seek out shops selling good, healthy food which is organic and produced by people that care. Stop picking up the first thing that you see. Look around. Do you know that all these chemicals in your food and cleaning products can cause cancer? Seek out healthy and ecological alternatives. Choose to have a happier, healthier life.

Now, back to body image.

If you have made changes and still feel it is difficult to love yourself, ask yourself, who taught you to view yourself as not beautiful and special?

We Angels want you to realise that if anyone has filled you with these ideas, it was because **they** thought those things about themselves. This is **not** about you.

Unhappy people try to rid themselves of their unhappiness by putting it on to you.

Once you all reconnect to your Soul and realise what pure, wonderful, loving and PERFECT beings you are, you will not need to repeat these patterns of behaviour.

When filled with self hate or low self-esteem regarding your appearance say,

"Please Angels, take away my low self image now. Clear me of all negative thought patterns. Restore me to my real truth and let me see myself for how I really am. A wonderful, beautiful, unique and perfect being."

Imagine the Angels showering you with white light from way above. This light is special and like all pure light, comes from the realms of the Angels. It is their special 'Angel-light'. As it washes you, it surrounds you, protecting you from all judgement from others and yourself. It goes into every cell, healing you. It goes into your mind, removing all those negative thought patterns. It goes into your skin, radiating it with beauty. This light illuminates your soul so brightly, that the wonder, beauty and perfection that is **you** shines out into your world, every second of every day."

Please dear Soul, do this as many times as needed, as often as needed. As you start to see yourself and your true beauty you will be amazed.

You will see yourself as we see you. Others will see you too. Those who see your true perfection will be your greatest allies, for these friendships that you form will be based on truth, not falseness and you will know a greater happiness than you have previously known. Keep a journal of your progress and read back on it, to further boost your esteem.

We Angels are with you always and we love you very much and want you to know just how special **you** really are. x

CHAPTER 20. FORGIVENESS.

When you remain in a place of 'unforgiving', because of the hurt you have experienced, which you perceive is too great to let to go, you keep yourself in a negative state, bound to the hurt.

The 'hurt' was in the past and we Angels want you to move forward to a better place, without the hurt robbing you of a happy life.

We want you to embrace forgiveness. To empower and heal yourself. We by no means, want you to allow yourself to be hurt by anyone and, we want you to know, it is not acceptable to allow yourself to be treated badly. The first step in freeing yourself and freeing yourself of the pain, is through forgiveness no matter what the circumstances were.

For example, you were in a relationship where your partner treated you badly and you are stuck. You are now afraid to enter into another relationship, as this memory has made you afraid.

Firstly, by the law of attraction, if you are afraid to enter into a new relationship, fearing more of the same, that is exactly what you will attract. According to the law of attraction, where you put your thought and feeling is what becomes your reality.

Secondly, you may think that you are only forgiving the perpetrator of your misery, when in fact you will also be forgiving yourself for allowing it to happen. Subconsciously, you are thinking, how could I have been so stupid to not see that this person was wrong for me?

Another good example where forgiveness may be required, is damage to your confidence or self esteem by a parent, caused either by their unhelpful guidance or absence and/or lack of love.

We want you to be healed, whole and free to fully enjoy your life. Enjoyment of your life is one of the reasons you chose to reincarnate.

We want to help you release the hurt that is holding you back. We want you to be healed and whole. We want you to spend a second focusing on your hurt and pain and the situation that brought it about, then we want you to say,

"I release to you dear Angels, the pain of the memory of this hurt. I forgive (insert name of person who has hurt you) and I forgive myself, with utter love.

Angels, take this pain and hurt from me now. Please fill me with forgiveness so that I may be able to enjoy life again. "

Imagine yourself showered with white light from above, that turns golden. Imagine this golden light filling your heart and radiating golden light out. Imagine your golden light/heart healed and imagine yourself at peace, with all the pain now removed from you.

Know that we Angels have healed your heart.

Know the only way to enjoy your life is to rid yourself of this pain, that you have been carrying for too long. Feel the golden light in you and around you and know that you are now free. Please do this exercise as many times as you need because dear Soul, you were meant to have a happy, loving and fullfilling life and the past has now been healed. Forgiveness heals **you** always. With our love - your Angels x ☺

CHAPTER 21. SUCCESS.

Success is not a word to be exclusively used in the pursuit of material achievement or as a gauge to measure material achievement.

Success is a measure of all achievement. It is personal to each individual.

There is only one way to be successful and that is to constantly monitor moments of success. Acknowledge them and praise yourself for noting them and be thankful that you had them. Thank yourself for making them happen. Thank the universe for bringing you those moments of success.

The reason that noticing your success (however small) not only alerts you to the fact that you have had success and are successful, but by the law of attraction, instantly increases the flow of success into your life.

So dear Soul, the only way to be successful is to

notice and acknowledge all your successes, however small.

Success is having a desire to do something and achieving it. What did you want to do that you have achieved?

Did you go and make a cup of tea or coffee when you wanted one? Was it delicious?

Did you go out on a date with that girl or boy you wanted to when you were young?

Did you go to the job interview?

Did you make a dream come true no matter how small or large? OF COURSE YOU DID!

We have all made a decision to do something and have done it! The problem lies in us **not** acknowledging that we have achieved.

Once we have achieved we moved on to the next desire or goal.

Only when you stop and notice your achievements, only once you honour your successes, then and only then will you be fully successful and enjoy your successes even more.

Sometimes you think that your success is small and insignificant because you are comparing your level of success or achievement to someone else.

This second you ARE successful because you have remembered all of your successes. By the law of attraction, when you notice and acknowledge your successes, you will attract more of them into your life.

Find out what you want. What is your goal for today, for this week or for this month? Then acknowledge that goal and make it happen but please notice your success when it does.

Success will not make you happy alone, because

as each goal or desire is realised and achieved, a new goal or desire will replace it. That is good! It is good to have goals and achieve them, but noticing when you achieve them, will make you feel really good! It will make you Joyous!

If you pin your happiness on just success you will never be happy, because the goalposts constantly move. What **will** make you happy, is knowing that you **are successful** and can achieve anything you wish to.

There is nothing different from you compared to anyone else on this beautiful planet of yours! There is nothing different from you compared to anyone else who is successful.

You are the same energy. You have the same capability. The only difference are thought patterns.

Successful people know that they are successful. They notice each success, no matter how small and honour it, therefore they bring more success into their lives.

We want you to be happy **now!** Go and buy a blank notebook and write from your earliest memory to the present day of something you wished to have or achieve. Write what it was (no matter how small) and when you achieved it, and then continue to enter your successes in this manner. Take pride dear Soul in just how successful you are! ☺

CHAPTER 22. Happiness & Joy.

I think we should also call this section live your dream now! We have noticed that many of you beautiful souls compare your joy to what others are doing and we want you to know that you can be joyous right now!

There is a legend of Arthurian Knights who sought 'The Holy Grail'. They spent many years wandering through bleak landscapes, forever in search of a mysterious Holy Grail, which they thought would bring them all the wonder and joy that they so desperately wanted. Their life was peaceful. They had friendship, love and a beautiful place to live, with food and riches. So why did they go off in search of the very thing that they already possessed?

Perhaps dear Soul, it is time for you to assess your life and realise how far you have come on your journey, how much you have achieved and how many obstacles you have overcome.

We angels suggest, that in order to have more of

what you want (according to the law of attraction, what you think and feel brings more of the same) you realise that you do indeed **already possess** your Holy Grail. That indeed you already possess all the happiness you want and by acknowledging it **regularly**, you will increase it **vastly.**

Thought of lack only brings more lack. Thought of happy feelings and gratitude brings more feelings of happiness, therefore bringing you even more to joyously express gratitude for!

We suggest you 'live the dream', rather than wait for it! We are not suggesting that you misinterpret this to mean that you spend all your money on a holiday, for example and are then miserable, but actually live the dream, in your heart and mind first.

What would you like to do, have or be if money, health or time was no object?

Once you become aware of what it will take to make you happy, you will be able to think of it and manifest it, by being aware of it and by thinking of it often.

Remember what you think today becomes your reality tomorrow.

The law of attraction brings to you what you think. As you start to have pleasurable thoughts in thinking, you will realise that your JOY has already started.

Simply by having happy, joyous thoughts about your wishes, you will realise that your happy, joyous thoughts **are** JOY. EnJOY thinking these pleasurable thoughts and as you become aware that these simple thoughts are pleasurable, you will realise instantly you are experiencing JOY and happiness, just by simply thinking about them.

This may be new for you but your joy and happiness can be instant with a simple thought.

Isn't it easy? Isn't this so much easier than you expected it to be?

Pat yourself on the back and praise yourself because you are changing and experiencing the wonder of your new life immediately.

More joy attracts even more joy!

You were given dreams to make them happen.

You will make your dreams happen.

You will manifest them, and then you will have new dreams to aim for. This is natural progression at force.

Don't be afraid to say what you want, then **think** about what you want. It is not what **others** want that is important in your world, it is what **you** want in your world which is important to you.

What you have always done, in the way that you have always done it, will only bring about the results that you already have. What you have always thought, by the law of attraction, will only bring you more of what you already have.

Isn't it time dear Soul to try something different? Try a different thought which will lead to a different result. Thoughts and feelings shape your future. Thoughts make your reality. Why not try happy thoughts that bring you joyous results?

We know change can be hard for some of you. You have lived for a while now with your thoughts and beliefs. As you start to think differently, choosing different thoughts that please and comfort you, you will manifest lives that please and comfort you.

Know each new thought brings your future. Feel safe in the knowledge, that we Angels are constantly supporting you, as you make these changes to bring you greater JOY in your lives.

The second you ask us to help you make changes in your life, to bring you greater JOY, we are with you, helping you.

We ask you to say,

"Dear Angels, please take my limiting thoughts now. Please guide me to live a happy and joyous life. Now!

Please make the transition from what I currently think, to what I need to think, in order to shape my life to its highest good. Dear Angels, help me to think and live differently so that I easily attract a happy and joyous life.

Dear Angels, give me the courage to follow the steps you lay out for me to follow, for my highest good now!"

Then imagine yourself showered with white light from above, protecting you. Imagine this light turning golden and showering you, in you and around you, entering into your thought patterns and literally en**lightening** them.

Now see yourself on a new golden path and know that it is good and right for you to be on this new path, which is JOY.

This path leads you to more JOY. Imagine a golden light going through you and into the ground, grounding you and securing you to this beautiful earth, for this is our gift to you, so that you may lead the wonderful life that you so deserve.

Our earthly friend Laura, who is writing this book, as we channel these messages to her, has spent fifty three years believing that she was stupid and useless because her father told her so.

She proved herself in the business world and made her many customers happy by creating beautiful jewellery for them.

Yet she still believed that she was stupid and useless, because her father told her so often.

She now believes that he was trying to push her into becoming successful, but all it achieved was to drain her of her confidence and self esteem.

She has now forgiven him, realising he knew no other way.

We lovingly gave her the help that she asked for, so that she could shape her life as she wanted it to be.

She still felt stupid and useless, so we constantly drew her attention to the many wonderful things that she has done and can do.

On her 53rd Birthday we channelled the information, that what you think brings your reality and she understood that in order to be happy and joyous, she needed to change her previously held belief that she was stupid and useless, into the thought that she was indeed clever, talented and capable.

She understood that changing her thoughts made her realise just how capable and clever she was. She fully understood our guidance and she now wonders how on earth she could have ever believed him and lived for so long with this sadness. It is important for her and us the Angels, that you don't wait a second more to realise that what you think and feel shapes your future.

It is easy for you to release old thoughts that are hindering you and holding you back.

First you have to realise which thoughts are holding you back.

Sometimes all you need is a different perspective on your situation.

A different perspective, leads to a different thought and that different thought will bring you the JOY that is rightfully yours.

That in fact the JOY was always there.

She wasn't stupid or useless and neither are **you**!

We want **you** all to realise that some of your previous thoughts may have been holding you back too.

Sometimes what other people tell you, holds you back from realising what wonderful, pure, wise, loving, perfect souls you are. We know, that you know this truth deep in your heart. You can do anything. So think and dream big. With our love, **your** Angels. X ☺

CHAPTER 23. AFFIRMATIONS.

Many of you may be aware that spiritual practitioners and alternative healing practitioners, advise you to say positive affirmations regularly. Often, you are not told how and why they work.

As we have already explained to you dear Soul, your thoughts create your future and what you think, by the law of attraction, brings more of the same.

This is all good and fine if you are thinking positive thoughts, which bring you more positive thoughts, which in turn bring you positive results in your life, but if you are in a place of worry or stress, it can be difficult to switch your thinking to more positive thinking immediately. We know that you need to think more positively, to attract more positivity in your life and these good, positive thoughts will go on to create your future.

Know that we Angels, want **you** to have the very best present and future, so when you are in a place of stress and worry, a fast way to immediately **halt** those negative thoughts and replace them with a positive one, is to say a positive affirmation.

The more you say them, the quicker you are changing your negative thought into a positive one. This will not only bring you good results but **make you feel better immediately**.

With practise you will be able to stop all negative thoughts of worry and stress by replacing them with thoughts that please you, rather than thoughts that only bring you more stress and worry.

By utilising positive affirmations, you will have positive and happy thoughts that will bring you a positive and happy life, with results that you will enjoy. You have to continue saying the positive affirmations even when things are good, to ensure that you get more good and keep the thoughts that do not please you, away.

As you become more aware of your needs, you will quickly be able to write your own positive affirmations which are personal to you.

Start by giving yourself praise.

See how that feels to you.

Then expand, write and say positive affirmations that make you truly happy. No one else need hear you say them. They are private to you, so please do not feel silly or embarrassed. Instead feel **empowered!** x

Here are some which we suggest... a few to get you started.

Please enjoy working with them, for this is our gift to you dearest Soul. X

Positive affirmations:

(Note that whilst saying them, you imagine yourself showered with golden light from above, washing away your fears and replacing them with all the positivity you need to have a beautiful life.)

I love myself totally and utterly. (Makes you smile immediately doesn't it?)

Every cell in my body knows how to heal itself. I AM strong and healthy.

I was created perfect. My essence, my soul is perfect. I AM still perfect.

(If you feel relief by saying any of these, you know that they are working for you!)

I AM loved by myself and others.

I AM safe and calm.

I let go into the arms of the Angels and all I need is always given to me.

This world is caring and safe. Every blade of grass knows how to reach for the sun and so do I.

I release all my previous limitations to the Angels. I AM safe.

I forgive myself. (Try repeating this one, a few times and see how great you feel.) If you cry, don't be afraid to let it out, it is all release and release is good. You are getting rid of all that limiting belief at last!

I let go of all guilt and shame now. I AM safe.

I AM successful.

I AM wise, capable and clever.

The Angels provide me with all the solutions that I need - ALWAYS! I AM safe.

I AM creative and can create everyday solutions for myself. I AM safe.

I AM beautiful and loved. I AM safe.

I AM happy and joy follows me everyday. I AM safe.

CHAPTER 24. RECEIVING GOOD THINGS.

Know dear Soul, no matter what happens in your life, good is always provided for you. As you fear and worry, you block the good coming to you, because you attract more fear and worry, by the law of attraction.

The simplest way to allow good, and good things coming into your life, is to let go of all the things that trouble you, then replace the space they took up with all good things.

So you ask - how do I let go of all the trouble, worry and fear? Simple, **just say it!** Say it **often** and know that the second you let go of fears, worries and troubles, they are gone!

If you find yourself filling up with more worry, fear and trouble, at a later date, **say it again**.

In fact, keep saying it, until all your fear, worry and trouble goes.

Know we Angels, want the best for you **always** and once you verbally and emotionally (that means actually **feeling** the 'let go' happen) let go of the fear, worry and troubles, you will be flooded with a sense of relief, which tells you it's gone.

Your feelings guide you, dear Soul. That is why you have them. Be kind to yourself. You may have had these feelings for a while and you are accustomed to them, but it is very easy for you to release these thoughts, fears and emotions that no longer serve you.

Most of the problems you experience here in the physical realm, can be healed and solved by only two things; releasing (letting go) and trust (knowing that when you verbally say I let go of… its gone) Trust is easier than you think and it happens very quickly.

The second you say, "I let go of all the hurt, pain and bad, and I allow good to come to me. I now give my self permission to have **all** the good the world has to offer", you start to feel better. You feel relief flooding through you. Know this and trust this. For it is the truth.

If you feel bad, by the law of attraction, more bad comes. So it is **your main job to feel good, expect good** and then you can know **more good is coming to you**, which in turn **will attract even more good,** by the law of attraction.

Here are some letting go/releasing exercises for you to say, in order to release your fear, worry and troubles. You can write your own too. Personalise them, so that they have resonance for you.

I let go of **all** fear and worry.

I let go of **all** illness.

I let go of **all** stress.

I let go of **all** that is holding me back.

I let go of **all** sorrow, guilt and shame.

Now say, "I relax into the arms of the Angels, I relax my head, I relax my neck, I relax my jaw, I relax my teeth, I relax my mouth, I relax my shoulders, I relax my arms, I relax my elbows, I relax my wrists, I relax my fingers, I relax my chest, I relax my heart, I relax my blood pressure, I relax my organs, I relax my stomach, I relax my genitals, I relax my hips, I relax my buttocks, I relax my legs, I relax my knees, I relax my thighs, I relax my lower legs, I relax my ankles.

I relax and let go.

I let go into the arms of the Angels. I let go and I am protected and safe and all I need is brought to me.

Always imagine yourself showered with white light from above, after releasing or letting go. Imagine this white light shower protecting and clearing you and going into your outer aura, and your inner physical body. Imagine it going into every cell in your body and imagine it going into your thought patterns, clearing and cleansing you, so that you are vibrating with white light.

Now imagine that light turning gold, in you and around you, from head to foot. Imagine that gold light coming from way up above, down, through you, surrounding you. Imagine you are golden light and golden light roots anchor you to earth grounding you.

Now let's fill up with good….

Say:

"I AM walking a magical golden path through life and I AM safe. Each step leads me to better and better experiences. The world is evolving and everyone is opening up to a greater love. We are all safe"

As you say this, feel it too.

Trust and believe it, for what you think and feel shapes your future, by the law of attraction.

Imagine you **are** golden light. It is in every cell of your body. In you, and around you.

Surrounding, and protecting you.

Imagine, that all the good, which is possible, is here for you.

Feel us the Angels, surrounding you and protecting you. Your own force-field of light. Protective beings, with you whenever you want us to be. Wherever you want us to be.

Just ask us to be with you and know that we are.

Feel the love that we have for you. Feel our love and connect with the pure love that is in every soul on this planet. Feel their love too, because each soul is pure, wise and loving, and your souls, are your own Angel within, made of the same stuff as we are.

See yourselves all radiating love to each other.

Feel the love wrapping itself through your planet and the universe.

See each inhabitant of the world radiating with golden light, golden love-light.

See this golden love-light dissolving all the dark negativity in the world. Be amazed that this light coming from **you** and **all** you beautiful souls, has the power to instantly dissolve any and all darkness. Feel your power, compassion and love.

See the light going into every animal, plant and human, every fish, tree and rock. See your beautiful earth, radiating with this golden love-light.

Now it's time dear soul for you to live your life

walking on your own golden path. We your Angels, want you to experience your life, as the joy that it is. X Enjoy. For we are always with you. XXX

CHAPTER 25. BRINGING PEACE TO THE WORLD.

In order to bring peace to the world, you need to reconnect with what loving peaceful souls you are.

We Angels are here to lovingly remind you that the energy you are is perfect in every way and made of pure love. Humanity is crying out to connect with that energy at the moment.

You are crying out to connect with your soul. This is why we the Angels are so accessible to you at this time. Your soul is your higher self, YOUR Angel within. This is the part of you that gets reincarnated. Your Soul chose your body, your physical human form, to come here to learn and experience life. However your physical body is not as advanced as your pure, wise, intelligent soul. You allow disconnection from your Soul. The good thing is, humanity is crying out to RECONNECT with your souls.

You have pushed your planet too far. You now want to rectify the mistakes humanity has made.

THIS IS A GOOD THING, as mentioned in the chapter about Manifesting. All you have to do is change your thoughts. It is human thought that creates and manifests wars. Remember thought comes first, then action. Your thought can change in an instant!

Once YOU start thinking about love, as opposed to fear, the vibration of the world will raise. It will rise quickly too, once you start realising that you are all made out of the same energy.

EVERY SINGLE ONE OF YOU IS MADE OUT OF THE SAME ENERGY!

Once you really FEEL and remember this, you will stop hurting each other. It is not natural to want to injure yourself.

Self protection is a NATURAL state. Once you realise you are all made out of the same wonderful and pure energy, you will stop hurting yourself and will realise hurting another is actually HURTING YOURSELF.

It starts with just YOU because as YOU awake to these truths, YOU start thinking of love, not fear. YOU realise we are all the same wonderful energy and changes happen instantly.

There are so many more of you out there that want change. That want peace! That is your real secret weapon.

Those who ARE reconnecting to their Soul realise that they are loving, peaceful and powerful.

YOU ALL ARE!

Don't think for one second, it is the ones who hold the guns who are powerful.

IT IS YOU WHO IS POWERFUL because there are millions more of YOU, than those that want war.

It is simply you have forgotten the law of manifestation, the law of attraction.

What you put your attention to becomes reality. What you think becomes your reality.

You can change your thought quicker than you can change your underpants.

So start thinking of love and peace. Start thinking

how good it would feel to have everyone holding hands, looking out for each other, being kind to each other and loving one another.

Remember Manifestation is: The Law of Attraction

THOUGHT/intention + FEELING/ emotion =

RESULTS.

It is **YOU** who is powerful. You pure and loving souls are all heroes. Xxx ☺

We will help you remove fear and anger from your world, all you have to do is ask us. Say, "Please Angels remove fear and anger from myself and our world now!" Know that it is done!

We can help you in so many ways. We cannot help you UNLESS YOU ASK US. We will not interfere in your lives because you have free will and free will is the basic human law of respect, freedom, honour and dignity.

We can show you how to help yourself. We can show you how to help your world. Just ask, we are always here, always waiting to help you. We are here to serve, here with love, for your highest good and the good of your beautiful planet. With our love your Angels.x☺

Part 2. Q. & A. Channelled answers to some of your big questions.

Here you will find some of your frequently asked questions, with answers channelled directly from the beautiful Angels.

Please remember to refer back to Chapter 4 - Channelling, advising you how to channel your own answers and advice from the Angels. With our Love x

1. Q. How can God do this? How can God allow wars?

A. God is not the one holding the guns. Humans are!

2. Q. What am I here for/what is my purpose?

A. You are here to learn and to teach others. You are here to give and receive love!

You are on this Earth to learn and to love.

Things that you perceive as challenges are opportunities for you to learn, grow and subsequently have happier lives.

Not all lessons will come to you as challenges.

Some lessons will come to you with great joy but know that even the challenges can bring you great joy, once you see the hidden opportunity to grow and teach others.

Do you notice how you all love Hero movies?

It is not the disaster you crave, it is the Hero overcoming challenges and saving the world that you love!

This resonates with the beautiful and perfect souls you truly are. You are all the Hero, if only you would realise it!

It **is** love that your heroic self uses to win battles not war. Love of your friends, your partners, your children and your pets. Love is your most powerful tool, as it soothes everything, heals everything and transcends time and space.

Are you not capable of loving those who are no longer here, as much as you did when they were here?

All you have to do is be open to love, time and time again, as love is the greatest, purest, energy there is.

Do not forget that you have an endless amount of love within you. If you feel a need to clear your heart of previous pain, ask us!

Say, "Dear Archangel Chamuel, heal my heart of past pain please and help me to open my heart to pure love again."

Imagine a golden light filling your heart. Then imagine pink rays radiating out from your heart into the world, touching everything and everyone.

The pink rays will shine back to you and as **you** are part of everything, **you** will receive this perfect love too.

Forgive all those who you perceive have hurt you. Forgive them often!

When you feel hurt it is an opportunity to remove from your life the things that cause hurt.

The hurt indicates what you do or do not want in your life.

Make allowances for everyone you come into contact with. They have forgotten that they are wonderful high vibration souls, full of love, peace and goodness.

Know too, that they have had life experiences with people who have not taught them this truth.

Possibly you are born to teach those people that

truth!

Sometimes you expect them to teach you about the wonderful being that you are but you have to allow forgiveness for them when you realise that no one taught them the truth either.

Share with each other, what truly wonderful Souls you are. You are made of the same stuff that made the world, made the universe, made the stars. You are all brothers and sisters because you are all made of the same stuff.

You are made of the same stuff as us the Angels. You are limitless and perfect **JUST AS YOU ARE.**

It is time to remember this and remind each other with love. Your love and ours.

The more you love, the more you learn from experience and compassion and the better lives you will all have.

Take pleasure in sharing your learning with others. Come together to inspire and support each other. Educate, not berate each other and go with love rather than judgement or hate.

Share love and support with each other and see the miracles occur in your lives. X

3. Q. How could you let my loved one die?

A. You are all here for a set time!

You have all reincarnated for a set time here on this planet. You knew how long you were coming here for, before you reincarnated. As you age you forget these facts.

Society currently informs you that you do not know these facts. As your world raises it's vibration and many more of you open up to your soul and it's wisdom, things that humanity has forgotten, will be remembered.

Much of your world is becoming more aware of reincarnation, through mediums and the fact that television, films and books are now providing you with the answers you have requested.

It is good that you are questioning.

It is your questioning that has accelerated these answers for you, for your empowerment, and evolution.

Many of you are in turmoil when your loved ones die because you feel you missed the opportunity to clear the air with them, tell them you love them or get closure on parts of your life-experience together.

You feel that because they are no longer **physically** present in your life, they are no longer present.

Know that this is not the truth. Know the truth. All energy exists at the same time and they are with you in energy/spirit form and know that you can talk to them at any time. Please realise that you can feel their presence any time **you** wish to.

4. Q. Please explain the law of attraction in respect to manifestation a bit more Dear Angels. I don't quite get it?

A.

We inform you that:

THOUGHT/intention + FEELING/ emotion =

RESULTS.

What you **think** and **feel** brings more of the same, by attraction into your life. You often do this with things you fear too. We Angels, are trying to guide you to only bring into your life things you actually want. So dear Soul, simply stop thinking about or imagining things you do not want, like war or illness.

Another way to think of this is:

WANT, BELIEVE, IMAGINE, ENJOY!

1. WANT.

So whatever you **want**, you have to **want** it, **really want it!**

2. BELIEVE.

You then have to **believe** that it is possible for you to have it.

It doesn't matter at first if you don't believe you can have it. You simply start to imagine that you **believe** you can have it.

3. IMAGINE.

Imagine what it **is** like to have it. **Imagine** what it **feels** like to have it.

4. ENJOY!

Enjoy the feeling of having it in your life. Basically imagine **enjoying** 'it' and 'it' will come. So many people get what they don't want because that is what they focus on and by thinking about it, the worry becomes true or the illness manifests.

IT IS **SIMPLE!** ONLY THINK ABOUT WHAT YOU **DO** WANT. The minute you start to imagine or think about what you don't want, change your thought.

Practise this now: Think of a **cat**. Now think of a **tree**.

How fast and easy is that?

You do not need to be frightened or panicked because it is easy to change your thought.

It is actually immediate. If you are afraid say, "Archangel Michael, protect me now and hoover away my fear and negative thoughts." Know that it is done.

5. Q. Is it reasonable to want to be happy all the time?

A. Yes!

Yes, it is reasonable to want and indeed expect to be happy all of the time. It is your right to be happy and contented, as your soul is made of pure energy. Your soul's natural state is that of total peace, total love, and total joy.

When you measure your happiness against what you have, you limit yourself. You say I will be happy when... I get rich, get thin, get married, have kids, see my kids grow, have more money, get a better job/house and so on.

You are constantly moving the goalposts. Aim to be happy now. Some of you are very happy indeed but perhaps don't even realise that you **ARE** happy.

You have a tendency to judge your happiness in comparison to other people's lives.

Understand that it is wonderful to want a bigger house, a better car, your family to be well and happy. It is great to have dreams and make them come true.

You were meant to strive, have ambition and succeed. How else could you grow? It is not a true foundation of happiness. Happiness is yours now if you feel it.

The rest is a list, a bit like a shopping list of things you want and some things that you think you want.

It is fine to have a shopping list but that is not your essence of happiness. Your essence is happiness and joy!

The shopping list is just a list of things you want to bring into your life. Once more manifestation is a feeling of what you want and how enjoyable it feels to have those things.

Thought and feeling plus action equals results.

Your shopping list can be fulfilled easily once you realise that it can.

You concentrate too much on the lack of things in your life which then manifests more lack.

Happiness has nothing to do with your list. Happiness is the natural state of your soul.

Other parts of your shopping list are items that are easy to fulfil. For example a teabag which you don't even need to buy, you can just **ask** a neighbour for one.

So the things on your list are not relevant to making you happy when you realise that you can have them all!

When you realise you do not need to search for happiness, as it is within you at all times, you will all have perfectly happy lives. What you perceive you do not have is what you make real.

Perceive you can have it all and you will!

The fact that you are all perfect loving beings of joy is real.

It is our pleasure to help you all live a better life.

We love you and always will! Xxx ☺

I wish to thank Sparky (Helen) for all her help and support during this journey of learning on which we have travelled.

I also thank my beautiful Guardian Angel, Angel-line and all the other Angels who I have had the honour and pleasure to work with during the writing of this book. Thank you Angels for always being here with me.

Laura. X

ABOUT THE AUTHOR

Laura Marsh has been working with the Angels her whole life. She was aware of their protection and guidance but it was only in later years that she understood who was helping her.

Since an early age people have always felt the urge to tell Laura their problems. This seemed strange to her at first, as often they were much older than she was.

The advice she gave always comforted and she knew a higher force was guiding her and 'telling' her the words needed.

During times of high stress Laura started communicating with the Angels regularly. The Channelled Angel messages she has received (almost daily) over the last sixteen years, have helped her navigate her way through life.

In November of 2015 she started getting specific, different messages set out in a book format. Laura was instructed to share these loving and healing messages in this book.

London born Laura, has been an artist and Silver/Goldsmith for the past 30. Years. She now lives in Scotland.

Look out for our new range of empowering merchandise to uplift & inspire.

www.angels-help-me.com

NOTES

Lightning Source UK Ltd.
Milton Keynes UK
UKOW06f1936030717
304605UK00008B/390/P